I0412271

The 50 Anti-Poverty States of America

Emotional Relief For Middle Class And Broke Americans

J.M. Seligman

Printed by CreateSpace: Charleston, South Carolina

Available from Amazon.com and other online stores

Available on Kindle and other devices

ISBN: 1490464794
ISBN-13: 978-1490464794

Printed in the United States of America

DEDICATION

I dedicate this book to all Americans who have struggled during The Great Recession. The 150 Million Americans living in or near poverty and the 50 Million Americans suffering from hunger in 2013.

CONTENTS

ACKNOWLEDGMENTS

I want to thank two Americans who provided relief, sense, and reason for me during a time that does not make sense. Thank you Tavis Smiley and Cornel West for your insights and honesty during The Great Recession.

I also want to thank my family, The City of Columbus, Columbus Jewish Family Services, Columbus Food Pantry's and Shelters, Columbus Metropolitan Library, and especially Craig Long for supporting me through these tough times. Last but not least, the Muse, Writers, Poets, and American Artists that cross my path every day.

"Be a warrior and love life…"

-Chelsea Light Moving

Introduction

"The economic depression which started in 1929 brought misery to millions of people, but let us not forget that the experience brought many blessings, not the least of these being the knowledge that there is something infinitely worse than being forced to work. It is being forced not to work."

　　　　　　　　　　　　　- Napoleon Hill

Let's take an hour break from this Great Recession with the "50 Anti-Poverty States of America". We are in a very difficult time in US history let alone world history. This Great Recession has been a great equalizer for all economic classes and a great destroyer of individual's lives. What is happening to all of US now?

I will primarily focus on the effects of the Great Recession in the United States and how it has affected my life. What I aim to provide is, a new set of attitudes to feeling better from this Great Recession and why this is happening. There are some factors that are unique to the 21st Century. I believe we can find new solutions while dismissing some of the myths about poverty.

I understand most people don't want to look at this and only want to look at the "sugar" in life. I completely understand and know the fear and pain can be overwhelming lately. We have lost a lot of sugar since 2007. The question now is, how are we going to bring the good life back? This book strives to bring the sugar back today.

It is about finding relief from the frustrations and the enormous emotional pressure we are all under. One of my friends recently said, "Maybe your book will show people how easy it is find these solutions again?" I hope so and my thought is, there are many Americans in the past who have laid a foundation for US. I have been pleasantly surprised at the "sweetness" this research has brought to my life.

The United States is the wealthiest country in the world, yet since 2007, we have one of the largest poverty rates in the industrialized world. The difficult truths of the Great Recession are income inequality, lack of work, and the lack of anti-poverty safety nets in 2013. It has split up marriages, families, and all relationships gay or straight. The new faces of American poverty are white, black, yellow, and red. It is everyone. We can't use superiority or racism as the cause for poverty any longer.

A new cause is, I am sad to say, 400 of the wealthiest Americans have the same amount of money as 150,000,000 Americans combined. This equals 400 Americans wealth for 50% of Americans wealth. This new income inequality is coming from a second industrial revolution, called the Financial and Information Revolution.

Why should we care about poverty? "That is in other countries or in our inner cities, they just need to try harder", is what we commonly hear. This shift is creating a new trend where there is a drop in average hourly wages from $20-$26/hr. to $9-$13/hr. These new jobs will naturally put Americans in poverty levels at $18,000-$25,000/yr. This means increasing poverty levels for all American towns and cities.

According to the book, "The Rich and The Rest of US" 85 percent of new job creation will be under 33 K per year while the top earners income levels will continue to increase. If this is true, then a national discussion on poverty is needed. So let's start talking about this new trend where trying harder won't be enough.

Not since the end of the 1800's have we seen these levels of wealth and income inequality in the United States. It was called the "Gilded Age" from 1877-1910. Today we have a new "Gilded Age" that started around 1979- to the present time of 2013. In 1995, the extreme wealth generated what was called a new, "Golden Age". This wealth imbalance is also creating cultural destabilization.

The difference between then and now is in the past; citizens, the wealthy, and the government took steps to balance this trend. Why aren't we doing that now? This is the reason for my book. I wanted to share what I have found for some emotional relief. It is not easy living in the 21st Century with growing poverty and income inequality during our current Gilded Age. How can we make our American hearts feel better?

In my anguish from unemployment and underemployment, I found new Anti-Poverty attitudes that have worked in the past and again today. I call them, "The 50 Anti-Poverty States of America", for all people that have fallen into poverty or near poverty since 2007. This includes the middle class, lower class, the working poor, and the generational poor of the United States.

I can't guarantee work, but I can direct you to proven principles for the past 70+ years that have created wealth consciousness. This book is a beginning to feeling better by looking at our US history and adding some helpful slogans. No one deserves to have the nightmare of poverty brought upon them just over a little bit of money. The Great Recession has some different dynamics that need to be looked at also, so here we go...

My concerns come from being raised in an upper middle class neighborhood in suburban Philadelphia. There was an attitude that if you worked for it, you could have it. The promise of America was that you do all the right things, and it will work out.

Growing up, I was aware that not everyone had money but I was fortunate to live in an environment where money was not a problem and all of our basics and then some were provided for. Many of the families had servants, nannies, or cleaning ladies.

As long as you educated yourself, worked for it, worked together for it, and planned you would be okay, if not well off. It was a time and place of material abundance and comfort. It was also during a time of prosperity in the United States, the 1970's and 1980's.

When I went to college it was really the first

time that money became something that really had to be earned. I went to college around Pittsburgh which was the center of wealth for the US Industrial Revolution. While living there, I got to personally see the mansions and excesses left from that era.

I learned the value of money as a poor college student like everyone else. This was also during the 1990's and the last decade of what I call the 2nd American Enlightenment. During the 1990's we really looked at the meaning of life due to the AIDS crisis, divorce, urban violence, crack, and then to counter balance that was the music scene. We had 5 different music scenes that blossomed from 1988-1996 of hip hop, industrial, techno, grunge, and the Manchester scene.

We talked Art, Nature, and Man and where we stood in the Universe. The New Age Movement and alternative medicines took off as well. Everybody went spiritual and looked at their relationship with each other and nature to have a healthier and better life experience. If everything was falling apart around you, what could you really hold onto?

During this time, there was always work, a way, and people to help you. Protections were lifted on Wall St. and deregulation was in swing. So there was an explosion of wealth that has never been seen before. They say the

US made $34 Trillion in profits. This is more than all of the World Kingdoms historically combined. So life was good all over. This was during the end of the Era of Love and Peace. Gasoline was cheap and if there were problems in the city from urban violence or drugs, you could get a job and move away to a better place with new people.

After college I moved to Columbus and had temporary jobs where I was able to take 3 and 4 day weekends and travel all over the United States. It was a great party of Art, raves, hardcore punk shows, music festivals, environmental awareness, and FUN! I traveled from NYC to Miami to Dallas to Los Angeles. Then from Madison east back to Philadelphia where I grew up. I was able to get involved with the youth cultures in all of these great cities along the way and felt a sense of safety and community as an American to other Americans.

Then I moved to New York City in 2001. Little did I know how much the United States and the World was about to change? I believe now, that our time of Peace from 1975 ended in 2001. I had traveled one quarter of the world by then; from London, England to Melbourne, Australia with North America in between. I was cosmopolitan, bi-lingual, well read, well dressed, and excited about life and the future. Then the 9-11 disaster came while I

7

was living in New York City.

If I have learned anything since 2001 it is how to manage my emotions and try and stay positive no matter what. I learned Nations have peace times, recessions, depressions, prosperity, and war times. The US had left a peace and prosperity time. I was able to emotionally handle the changes until The Great Recession started in 2007, and then it became a completely different ball game. **Economic depressions are hard.** They have never been easy to get through.

I really had to focus, re-learn, re-balance, and completely change my thinking to adjust to the times. I have never felt so bad about myself in my life since The Great Recession. Sometimes I compare it to being in a war, with that being the only thing worse than an economic depression. Now I think I know what it must feel like to be under siege sometimes, stuck in the house!

What I hope to leave with you is a quick guide to bounce out of all of those bad feelings. What has made matters worse are the public's, states, and federal leader's negative attitudes about poverty. I completely understand that no one wants to look at something so scary but we need to end our disconnect as to why this is happening. Many people and families are really struggling now. What else can we do to emotionally handle The Great Recession? Do we need to make this worse than what it already is?

There is nothing wrong with you or any of US going through this difficult time in American and World history. I am just tired of the guilt, shame, and blame of my circumstances.   I find it interesting that before 2007, I was this great guy because I was working all the time, then magically after the work went away I am just this terrible person? If anything I have become a stronger, more resilient, and innovative American since The Great Recession and new work trends have started. I hope my story will show you that you can get through this too.

With my down time from unemployment I have discovered something new, something so surprising, and wonderful about life. I think this new information can be useful to you or anyone struggling during these tough economic times. I feel it can really help us get out of all these negative thoughts, negative feelings, or grasp of the devil if you want to call it that? I discovered that spiritual solutions and history can help us for these 21st Century demands.

Where do we begin? First we need to feel better and I hope to add some relief to your life. This book is for the middle and lower classes that have slid into poverty (new poor), the working poor, and the generational poor. Poverty was such a "bad" word during our era of prosperity 1979-2007, but that time is over now.   We need to re-define what poverty means in the 21st Century.

I have spoken with the richest and have spoken to the humblest of Americans. It seems everyone is going broke from outside forces, so we are all equal. The Financial Collapse of 2008 came and wiped out ½ of all monies in the United States and around the world. Now a large majority of US are living in poverty, all classes, physically and mentally, while income inequality increases.

Personally, I think I have fallen as low as I can go emotionally and the only place we can go now is UP! So let's get up and pay it forward. Let's share these "50 Anti-Poverty States of America" to work together and get out of these terrible circumstances that the general public did NOT create for ourselves.

The Gilded Age and the Great Depression were the only other times in US history that were as bad as this; without war. Some say 60 percent of Americans were struggling with poverty in the 1930's and The Great Recession was at 50 percent in 2012.

I remember seeing an anti-poverty day on TV with Tavis Smiley and Cornel West while I was unemployed. They had national speakers throughout the day speaking about how so many Americans are wrestling with poverty since the Financial Collapse. I picked up their book, "The Rich and the Rest of US" and it inspired me to write about what I have been going through myself.

These are my thoughts and feelings about what I have seen and lived through since 2007. I wanted to add on to the discussion of American poverty and hunger in these tough times. How then do we begin to feel better so we can do something about this? Let's take a look now at what I have found to, emotionally, turn these challenges around.

The 50 Anti-Poverty States of America

What are these?   I love the idea of positive affirmations for our day. When I was a child I remember seeing posters of anti-racism and anti-sexism sayings at my Grandparents house in New Jersey. Even though I grew up in Philadelphia, New York City and northern New Jersey were always second homes to me. What is different about those two big cities are their public transit systems. There were a lot of posters, Public Art, and Public Service Announcements to help everyone.

You could always see something creative about our culture whether it was helpful or aggravating, whether polished or graffiti. These announcements were primarily for anti-violence, anti-drug, anti-HIV, and most recently anti-terrorism. It was a way to help the public get through a common threat or bad situation.

The Great Recession is a common threat and a bad situation and where are our helpful messages for this? So I stayed up many nights and came up with the "50 Anti-Poverty States of America". Now we can have Anti-Poverty and Anti-Hunger posters up at the bus and train stations as well. These daily slogans are to clear our minds and hearts of the frustrations from this painful time.

I wanted to create something that I could use to focus on during the day while I was looking for work. I needed something to take the pressure off the grind of "applying and trying". These slogans or affirmations brought me relief and I hope they do you too. What helped me most was focusing on one or two slogans for the day to keep my spirits up.

Did this come from something locally? Yes, Columbus most recently got involved with public art at their bus stops also. Our public transportation system had a culturally German inspired program called, "Reinigungegesellschaft" or The Cleaning Society. (Seman Jr., 2012) Yes, that is what I said?!

It offered future forward ideas for city residents around transportation and the environment. Their slogans inspired me to come up with my own for poverty and hunger to get out of this Great Recession emotionally.

No. 1

American Frustration
to
American Food

No. 2

American Disturbance
to
American Decency

No. 3

American Guilt
to
American Good

No. 4

American Catastrophe
to
American Clothing

No. 5

American Denial
to
American Dialog

No. 6

American Hatred
to
American HELP!

No. 7

American Classicism
to
American Care

No. 8

American Racism
to
American Renewal

No. 9

American Homophobia
to
American Honesty

No. 10

American Sexism
to
American Safety

No. 11

American Ignorance
to
American Interest

No. 12

American Mean
Spiritedness
to
American Marshall Plan

No. 13

American Recession
to
American Re-Birth

No. 14

American Swindle
to
American Shelter

No. 15

American Foreclosure
to
American Forgiveness

No. 16

American Despair
to
American Declaration

No. 17

American Unemployment
to
American Unity

No. 18

American Financial
Collapse
to
American Financial
Freedom

No. 19

American Shame
to
American Security

No. 20

American Blame
to
American Believer

No. 21

American Bullying
to
American Bravery

No. 22

American Poverty
to
American Promise

No. 23

American Problems
to
American Pride

No. 24

American Bankruptcy
to
American Better Life

No. 25

American Injustice
to
American Innovation

No. 26

American Anger
to
American Answers

No. 27

American Viciousness
to
American Vision

No. 28

American Judgment
to
American Justice

No. 29

American Criticism
to
American Critical Thinking

No. 30

American Lies
to
American Liberation

No. 31

American Nightmare
to
American Neighbor

No. 32

American Corporation
to
American Cooperation

No. 33

American Hostage
to
American Hospitality

No. 34

American Loss
to
American LOVE

No. 35

American Disappointment
to
American Direction

No. 36

American Deprivation
to
American Dessert

No. 37

American Insanity
to
American Introspection

No. 38

American Scare
to
American Solvency

No. 39

American Oppressed
to
American Optimism

No. 40

American Indifference
to
American Interdependence

No. 41

American Depression
to
American Drive

No. 42

American Police
to
American Peace

No. 43

American Prisons
to
American Possibility

No. 44

American Income Inequality
to
American Intelligence

No. 45

American Suffocation
to
American Survivor

No. 46

American Siege
to
American Solutions

No. 47

American Ruin
to
American Resources

No. 48

American Decay
to
American Determination

No. 49

American Greed
to
American Graciousness

No. 50

American Outsourcing
to
American Ownership

Hungry US Cities 2012

I have found some solace and refuge in the book, "The Rich and The Rest of US" by Tavis Smiley and Cornel West who also have a weekly national radio show. They put out their book after the, "Poverty Tour: A Call To Conscience 2011." They traveled throughout the Mid-West, North East, and the South to speak to all Americans and find out what was happening to them, during this Great Recession.

One fact stuck out to me while reading this book, that 50 million Americans are going hungry and aren't sure where their food will come from tomorrow, next week, or next month. That can't be is what I thought?! 1 out of every 6 Adults is going hungry according to the www.FeedingAmerica.org website. 1 out of every 5 children is going hungry according to a local radio station Public Service Announcement on 92.3 FM WCOL. On the

NBC World Evening news, they were mentioning how 25+ million Americans were unemployed in 2012, so 50 million hungry is not out of the question.

All I know is that I never went hungry until after 2007. Yes, maybe once or twice before that for 1 meal, but not like the days, weeks, months, and years of figuring out my food like I have had to since 2007. What does 50 million people really look like? So I went to the US Census Bureau for the year 2011 and pulled up some figures. If we look at some well-known US cities I believe we can understand the scope of this Great Recession and new low wages trend much better.

What I have learned is if we take the populations of some of our greatest cities and add them up, it produces a list. These city populations do NOT cover the surrounding suburbs. So let's say, we know Pittsburgh is a large city around 2.3 million with suburbs, but in the July 2011 census it is around 300,000 for residents **inside** the city limits. So I added up all of the cities populations to 50 million Americans. I feel this list gives a more realistic view as to what is REALLY happening to US all. Let's look and see if we can start to develop more compassion for our fellow Americans and co-workers.

If 50 million Americans are going hungry tonight, what would this look like in the United States cities 2012-2013?

1. New York City
2. Los Angeles
3. Chicago
4. Houston
5. Philadelphia
6. Phoenix
7. San Antonio
8. San Diego
9. Dallas
10. San Jose
11. Jacksonville
12. Indianapolis
13. Austin
14. San Francisco

15. Columbus (Hello!)
16. Fort Worth
17. Charlotte
18. Detroit
19. El Paso
20. Memphis
21. Boston
22. Seattle
23. Denver
24. Baltimore
25. Washington D.C.
26. Nashville
27. Louisville
28. Milwaukee
29. Portland
30. Oklahoma City

31. Las Vegas
32. Albuquerque
33. Tucson
34. Fresno
35. Sacramento
36. Long Beach
37. Kansas City
38. Mesa
39. Virginia Beach
40. Atlanta
41. Colorado Springs
42. Raleigh
43. Omaha
44. Miami
45. Tulsa
46. Oakland

47. Cleveland
48. Minneapolis
49. Wichita
50. Arlington
51. New Orleans
52. Bakersfield
53. Tampa
54. Anaheim
55. Honolulu
56. Aurora
57. Santa Ana
58. St. Louis
59. Riverside
60. Corpus Christi
61. Pittsburgh
62. Lexington

63. Stockton
64. Cincinnati
65. Anchorage

So if all the hungry people in the US were living in these cities, for the purpose of my EXAMPLE, this is what it would look like. It would mean **every single inhabitant of these 65 cities** would be hungry or not knowing where their next meal is coming from. That means there are Men, Women, Children, Veterans, Special Populations, the Elderly, and me in there! In reality, these 50 million Americans would be split between 1/3 city, 1/3 suburb, and 1/3 rural for where the hungry live.

This is not acceptable in any form, all the more reason to bring back anti-poverty programs again. Especially since our country produces enough food to feed half of the world. So why are we starving in the wealthiest country in the world? Why are so many of US hungry? I think it comes down to Denial of the problem in Washington D.C. and a broken economic system that produces Income Inequality.

No one should be going hungry in America as long as we can produce food. Not only can we produce food, but we can produce enough to feed most of the world! I read that all of Egypt's 83 million people are fed by the United States exports. Wow!

These hunger and poverty problems cause a threat to our very way of life, our National Security itself. I wanted to leave spiritual and historical "life lessons" in this book, to let people know we do not have to destroy everything. No, just 50 million people need some relief.   What can we do? We can start working together again. I like the idea of giving our fellow Americans a hand up and not a hand out. Whether the food comes from Charities or Government assistance, or any combination of the two. I suggest that we return to the anti-poverty solutions the US has already used to stop long term poverty. We do not have to continue this situation.

The last President to start new anti-poverty programs was Lyndon B. Johnson (1963-1969). He enacted a series of humanitarian actions with his "Great Society" and his War on Poverty. The poverty rates were 19 % in 1964 and in 2009 they were 20%+. All of the US Presidents since Richard Nixon have been cutting anti-poverty programs up to President Barack Obama. Were there other times in America where people were not in denial and wanted to help each other? Yes, and let's look at a few of those solutions.

21st Century Interdependence

This is only an introduction to my views as to a way of mending these tough times we are all walking through.   First of all the "50 Anti-Poverty States of America" are a pick me up. Now where is this coming from?

Simply put; I see something special from all of my studies on US history, Public Transportation Art, and Interdependence. Like I said earlier, the 1990's were a special time and something very important happened then. We were all reminded that we are all interdependent on each other and the Earth.

There is a human behind every product in your home, apartment, car, work, bicycle, the sidewalks we walk on, etc... Everything we touch and use for our daily activities, every day, was produced by someone else or the idea was made by them for you before a machine produced it. Plus, everything we need or use comes from the Earth. Simple enough.

Well in 2008 we had two major problems at once, a Global Warming Hurricane 1,100 miles north of the Ocean blowing apart my city with winds above 75 mph for 7 hours! It cost Ohio $1 Billion in damages. Then the Financial Collapse where man and woman's greed was more important than other human beings, the environment, or their nation's safety.

When we use the spirituality of Interdependence in our lives we realize everything everyone does can affect our lives. Yikes and hooray! People are our destroyers or they are our saviors. It just depends on their minds.

Unfortunately when people are under the influence of their egos, fears, and selfishness.. life can go terribly wrong. Which we have all seen across the United States with The Great Recession and new work trends. When we really look at life through the lens of interdependence life becomes more beautiful and abundant. If we are lucky, even a MIRACLE!

The spirituality of Interdependence in work and politics will equalize all peoples and put the Earth in the equation as well. This is the beauty of being a 21st Century World Citizen. I believe this attitude of Interdependence will solve the problem of the economy in the long run and Global Warming as well.

They said on National Public Radio in March 2013, that it will take 25 years to start a cooling process (2038) if we shut off all of our CO_2 production today. So we are in a pickle... It is a man-made pickle, not the Universe or the Earth, we did this to ourselves. This also means we can get out of it.

I am still upset over Super Storm Sandy 2012 that wiped out my summer vacation beaches from Fire Island, NY to Cape May, NJ. Cleveland, OH had waves from Lake Erie over 22 ft. tall flooding their city also. It is another summer destination of mine. My thoughts are with the victim's families that are still homeless or rebuilding from that triple storm which turned into a mega hurricane. Recently, my heart went out to the victim's families of the mega twister that hit Moore, Oklahoma 2013.

Then we have the big corporations where they can't see beyond their computers. It is so sad that many of these big corporations feel their "ends to their means" are more important than their own humanity and environment that sustains them, it even gave them life!

All I know is we came from the Sun and the Earth and we return to the Sun and the Earth when we die. What are we doing in between those two times? Why are we messing all of this goodness up with Poverty and Global Warming? There is plenty for everyone and we can have a comfortable climate as well.

I believe the first thing we have to do though is to stop the unkindness towards each other. We are all suffering from The Great Recession and Corporatism wreaking havoc across our great country.   One of my friends said, "I can't wait until this time ends."

What is Corporatism? I feel it is when success becomes greed and a complete disregard for people and the earth occurs. There is nothing wrong with working hard and becoming successful in what you do, but creating income inequality and misery physically and environmentally is a different story. Then add the threat of Global Warming on top of those problems. **Those attitudes just don't make any sense anymore for what we need to do in the 21st Century.**

Time will set right their wrongs as it always has. Like the ocean tide, water comes in and then it goes out. Unfortunately, in their flurry to control and have "power over", they are missing their day and this beautiful planet.

I would like to see the return of a time when we help each other get out of poverty,

Americans to Americans. Yes, there are good corporations or good big businesses that are philanthropists and are helping their workers and the environment.

I would also like the good big businesses to speak to the ones causing these problems because without economic stability and the environment, there is no business. Then you will lose your jobs as well and be right here with me.

We are currently at 50 percent for this new trend and have 35 percent more Americans to go; to work for lower wages. Where you will have to live through the throws of everything I am about to describe, with your own descent into poverty. It will only take high gasoline costs, new economic collapses, and low wages to send you on this tract. Natural laws always re-balance the off balance energy and we are out of balance.

According to the book, The Rich and The Rest of US, (Smiley & West, 2012) there are 150 million of US who are living in or near poverty since 2011, making 23-33k per year. They are saying 1 out of every 2 Americans is living in poverty now. A striking statistic with this is that 50 percent of Americans make $33,000 or less per year equaling that 150 million number. 70 percent of Americans make less than $57,000/yr. according to the IRS online Tax Filing 2013, www.irs.gov/uac/freefile.

I really don't like knowing that no matter how hard I try or with the education and skills that I have, I will only be able to live at or near the poverty line for my future, because that is what's available. Sure, there are always exceptions to the rule but when it is a major trend that is different. The likelihood that this Financial and Information Revolution will create a new "permanently poor" class is likely. What can we do instead?

The saddest thing about all of this is knowing I could have a better life if I moved to Slovenia now, because they have less Income Inequality. This is why I believe my book; the "50 Anti-Poverty States of America" can help.

During the last "Gilded Age" in 1890-1910, the wealthy, public, and politicians helped each other get through. We know the formulas for wealth and success in America. I wanted to show we can do that again based on a new 21st Century spirituality and some of the lessons from the 2nd American Enlightenment 1960-2000. I also wanted to celebrate the charities and organizations that are hard at work helping Americans already. Thank you for all your efforts.

Where can we find Interdependence? It has been a spiritual truth for many earth based cultures and religions around the world, East and West. Just go to the library or any book store and you will find it. I hope you can now see that we have American options and then some, to get our lives back on track.

The first step is to relax with the "50 Anti-Poverty States of America". Then we can start talking solutions again. Plus, it is much more fun, being part of a community or country, where we can share our humanity with each other. That is basically it for me. Emotional pain is just not our natural human state of being. Economic pain is not what the Founding Fathers had envisioned for US either.

My Story: The 50 Anti-Poverty States of America

First I would like to thank all the good people who have helped me. There has been love and goodness along the road since 2007 for me. Most importantly I want to thank my family, closest friends (too many to list), food shelters, and social agencies at the city and state levels.

Then I'd like to thank the Unitarians, Hindus, Buddhists, Christians, Native Americans, Muslims, Pagans, Atheists, and Jews that have fed, housed, or clothed me. I really like knowing everyone's God has been equally helpful during The Great Recession and this new trend. That is another reason why Americans are so great!

Now we will look at my trials and tribulations that have happened to me since 2007. I don't feel ashamed to share this because if it helps one person, then it was worth it. I wanted to share my decent into poverty during this Great Recession. Not to frighten you but just to let you know that, YOU ARE NOT ALONE, in some of these difficult, scary, or ridiculous situations. Down into the rabbit hole we go...

So I came from the American Upper Middle Class and with those values and became part of the American Creative Class as an adult. There are 40 million of us that are educated, talented, skilled, producing, and selling our products or services. I come from a high school which created some big names such as Josh Wink, Seth Green, and Kobe Bryant to name a few.

The Creative Class bounces from success to failure as any Artist does, but the faucet of money got shut off for me starting in 2007, like so many other Americans. Like I said earlier, The Great Recession is a great equalizer.

In 2007 I moved back to Philadelphia because Ohio had started their Recession one year before the rest of the US. That would be August of 2006 and by Christmas of 2006 the ways for me to support myself were gone. My two industries had stopped.

I used to live off of working in the hotels as a banquet server and selling my art work. I always had two jobs and it was nothing for me to work 60 hours a week between the two. I could make $14-18/hr. on average and up to $18-26/hr. with special parties. During the holidays I could make an extra $500-$2,000/ mo. from my paintings. This would allow me to have savings during the down times where I would produce my work and then sell it later to make more extra income.

Hanukkah/Christmas of 2005 I could work 15 shifts per week and Hanukkah/Christmas of 2006 I worked 5 shifts all month. What was happening here? So I moved back home to Philadelphia in search of more work for April of 2007. It was a tough year; I lost all of my belongings and my car due to the move and cost of living.

Before 2007 I was always able to find work or sell something I produced to make ends meet. Now that equation changed from light to dark. Economic disasters derail millions of people from their good lives and throw them into poverty.

I spent one year back home and made $24,000 working two jobs and commuting 3 hours per day. I wasn't able to work the entire year there, I think only 9 months. That was the last time I lived above the poverty line of $23,000. Then I returned to Columbus because of the East Coast high rents, lack of high wages, and big city violence.

Yes, everywhere has their ills of society. It was heartbreaking for me to leave home again, but it only made sense. I went back to my friends and Art community thinking I could start over and build up everything again. I had to keep it moving...

Shortly after I got back we had a time that changed me. September of 2008 was a moment where nothing in my life would be the same again. We had "Hurricane Ike" blow through knocking out all the power, wrecking much of the City of Columbus, and the State of Ohio.

I was frightened to my core and I had to call my sister in Philadelphia to get any news about the Hurricane on my cell phone. We had lost all electricity for 3-7 days in the city. That meant no TV, internet, newspapers, or telephones, unless your cell phone still had some electricity. It was eerie but the neighbors came together and we made the best of it. In fact we had some great barbeques. Unfortunately, my job didn't lose power, so it was MADNESS with the theft and shock people were going through. We got through it though.

Then the Financial Collapse the following week. So Capitalism ended and Global

Warming made itself known and gas prices were so high it was damn hard to travel locally. I knew from September 2008, we must do something different from this point on. I believe everyone will have two jobs for the 21st Century. One job in our personal time to reduce our CO_2; and two, to pay our bills during our professional time.

The Universe and Mother Earth made that known for humanity. So I wrote my book, "The Last Fill Up: Electric Bicycle Lifestyle Plans" to give people solutions to high gasoline costs and offer inexpensive ways to travel locally without polluting. Basically I found a way to have fun going to work or school while reducing our CO_2.

Well from 2008-2012 I was able to find work and have my own apartment again. I even bought a used car, bicycle, and an electric bike. I felt like I was getting my life back together. My job was less than desirable because I was underemployed and it was dangerous. The stresses of poverty were real but I was working.

Poverty will make you crazy if you are hungry, and do things that you wouldn't normally do. I had to go to food shelters the 4th week of every month for two years to make ends meet. During those two years, I was working full time 40hrs/wk. and going to food shelters to get by. Then there were the threats of urban violence, prostitution, and theft living in lower class neighborhoods.

What I realized was something new was descending, poverty, all over the city. It didn't matter what neighborhood you lived in anymore, someone was going to steal your stuff. That was new. It wasn't just me and my life path. This situation was happening to everyone. I heard of so many job layoffs and was grateful for my anything. The worst part of it has been the anxiety and fear of will this happen to me too?

From 2009-2011 I promoted my book and online biz idea. The apartment I was living in had its window shot out twice by teenage hoodlums with a BB gun. I promoted my business and met with over 2,600 people at local events, giving them my card or flyer, over a 3 year period. Then I got cyber attacked, hacked, and my on-line biz shut down. My e-bike got broken into and destroyed as well.

This was a really tough time for Americans and the entire World was what I learned from my experience. I felt a new despair and depression that I had never felt before.   What are we going to do if there isn't work here in my city, state, or country and other international companies are preventing me from working too? Then a local stole my bicycle?! Man, tough crowd, tough crowd.

Five months later I quit my job because of the stresses and threats of violence at the work place. None of this was acceptable but I felt it was the next right thing. No job is worth losing your life over. So I put my two weeks in and then a new wrecking ball started in my life.

I was not able to find full time work for 10 months and then that only lasted for 2.5 months. All 55 of us were laid off on a Friday. That was the longest I had been unemployed before having full time work since I was 15 years old. One of the men there used to make $70,000/yr. before the Financial Collapse, now he was living off of $20,000. That is a $50,000/yr. pay cut!   No wonder people have lost their minds and have become hateful.

One big miracle did happen though; I was basically given $2,000 from the spirituality of Interdependence to go to Mexico for 5 weeks. I went to learn more about my Art and another culture. Before I left I had $3 to my name for 3 months. Then when I got back, I had $6. One of my friends said, "Oh, so you doubled your money?"

I felt very fortunate and I met so many wonderful people. It was such a beautiful place and I met people from all over the world. What was interesting was, many of them were going through what I was going through. It was also scary to hear their stories about how hard it was for them in France, Spain, England, Germany, Finland, Canada, and other parts of Central or South America.

I realized this was a problem with the bigger economic system. This Great Recession was everywhere. When I was there a Mexican local said, "By 2020 the cost of living will be the same in the US as in Mexico. Mexico is going up while the US is going down and then all the Gringos will be coming here for work. We might start having Gringo illegals!" That was hilarious. Who would have thunk it? This is how much things have really changed.

I just felt grateful I had a minute to take a break from the pain. What made me the most aggravated was knowing I was having a normal middle class experience and that I may not have that opportunity again, due to the Great Recession and this new trend.

Needless to say, looking back, I lost it all in 2012. I lost my job, my apartment, my love, my gym membership, belongings, and car again. This was ridiculous, losing it all twice in 6 years, but that is what happened. I may not have lost a house to foreclosure but I have lost my home due to lack of work and money since 2007. I haven't been able to get back above the poverty line for 6 years. How can a man at the prime in his life, educated, talented, healthy, and wanting to work be going through such a thing?

Well everyone said the answer was from The Great Recession. I think the thing I resent most is; no guarantee for my basic needs anymore. It really takes an emotional toll applying for work, working, and then having all of your money taken away as soon as you get it. Then you have no abilities for savings or expendable income, it is no fun. Thank goodness for Ellen, The Voice TV show, and Netflix!

I remember talking to a friend and asked, "What is happening to me?" Her answer was, "Poverty". No I'm just broke, that isn't me and it isn't. I learned **"it isn't"** for 30 percent of the New Poor either. I was lucky to be able to stay at a friend's otherwise I would have become homeless. In high school I used to volunteer to help the homeless in center city Philadelphia, and now I had landed in a similar situation. All I know is that I was an athlete and you keep trying even if it hurts. Never give up.

What frightened me was if there was no hope of work, food, shelter, clothing, and transportation for a capable grown man, what about the vulnerable people? What about the elderly, the children, the veterans, the special populations? There must be something we can do about this?

When it comes to transportation, it is one of the largest issues revolving around poverty. The costs of transportation can make or break an individual or families food for the week. It can make or break a job interview or keeping the job. It can also prevent people from getting the resources they need if they do have the money to purchase them. I have gone through these situations too.

Transportation and my struggles with it have led me to alternative modes of travel, bicycling, electric biking, carpooling, and public transportation. If gasoline is too expensive or the car upkeep is too expensive on lower wages, what other options are there? The Great Recession and these new work trends have asked me to live and travel differently.

This was my taste of the Great Recession, it started and now I want to focus on how to get out of it. Then the news says the Recession was over in 2009, and Wall St. is back above pre-financial collapse levels? How do we reconcile this while there are still no jobs? Now they are saying the de-industrialization of America is the main culprit. Well then, where is the help needed to create new jobs to get out of poverty? There was a great article with a wage chart called, "Wages Stink At America's

Most Common Jobs". (Luhby, 2013)

Let's lighten things up a bit, now for some ridiculous truths from this time. I wanted to go to a live music concert for a favorite band of mine that was coming to Columbus. I couldn't afford the tickets so I bought a lottery ticket for $1 and got back $41. Yes, that covered the ticket and a beer to see two L.A. Bands, The Delta Spirit opened up for The Silver Sun Pickups.

Then I really wanted to go to a poetry slam but it cost $5 and I didn't have $5. So I took my housemates beer cans and went to the recycling center. I got $8 so I had a hot chocolate while there also. I never appreciated entertainment so much before. Then realized, well at least I still have my health, a sense of humor, and my mind.

The Hanukkah/Christmas season of 2012 was the worst in my life. It was so bad I can't even talk about it. I just felt like I was in that song by Everclear, " I Will Buy You A New Life". So I thought boy, can't wait to get out of 2012, let 2013 be better...

I thought nothing else could happen, and then it did... January came and with it the lowest points of my life, still "applying and trying" and nothing. Then everything got worse during the coldest darkest time of life, Winter.

Mid-Western winters are not kind either. My food stamps were cut off and I had to live off of $10/wk. for food for 3 weeks until they got turned back on. There is nothing like that burning feeling in your stomach when you are hungry. You haven't lived until you've stood at the bus stop in 5 F and hungry. Hunger hurts.

I was lucky, though; I got them back and got past that time. Since I am over 21, my family gives when they can give. But I just squeaked through and I couldn't even buy a cup of coffee. Learning how to live without wasn't pleasant but I did it. I thought, "It may not be easy right now, but I will find a way to get out of this unemployment".

My mantra all 2012 had been just buy coffee, bread, and butter and you're alright. Couldn't even do that anymore and then got sued for not paying my remaining credit card debt due to no full time work since November 2011. I paid them down for two years from my on-line business, and then I couldn't any more. The funniest thing was, they would all say while they were suing me was, "How are you getting by?" My answer was, "I'm not." All of this because I was trying to find work, create my own work, or provide work for my community...

By 2013 I had used up all savings, cashed in any assets, and sold off anything I could to make money. There was nothing left and my student loan payments were on economic hardship deferment. I looked into going back to school but I would need to pay my student loans for 6 months before I qualified for new loans to go back to get re-trained. Nope, no more options, no more safety nets, and no work to dig myself out. This was the end of the line, I was finished... I can't help but hear Tim McGraw's song, "Last Dollar (Fly Away)" in times like these.

Then I got a job interview in Pittsburgh but could not go, because I needed a job to get a job. The other thing that was interesting was they wanted to use my credit score in the hiring process for a $9/hr. + commissions job.   How can you have a good credit score if you are not working? I really feel credit scores should be illegal in the job hiring process. Who's going to have a good credit score after long term unemployment from The Great Recession and these new work trends?

Hopefully people will start to see beyond their stubbornness and "power over" that, this Great Recession doesn't discriminate and no one is safe from it. It has nothing to do with your age, class, race, religion, education, sexual preference, or work experience. If there are no jobs in your area, there is no work and no money to live. That is it! It is not a choice anymore of if I wanted to be successful or if I was really trying to find work. Can't we just help each other get back to work?

I guess the most frustrating thing is it seems the public and politicians have become blaming and self-seeking. Then the churches and social agencies are over-burdened and underfunded. What I hear is, "So what are you going to do about it?" I'd like to turn that around and ask what are WE going to do about this? This is a half of America problem not an individual one.

In my city and neighborhoods that I travel through on the bus, there was so much poverty, alcoholism, drug addiction, and threats of violence. I like knowing that there are more good people than bad people. So as long as I don't end up on the 6 o'clock evening news, I'm good.

Then, I was at a bus stop recently, and 8 gun shots rang out about 150 ft. behind me. Needless to say I am never going to that bus stop again. What happened to my America? Where are the promises of the country I was raised with?

This is a nightmare of national proportions. Then I fell into one of my worst depression of my life. I still applied for jobs Monday through Friday but if no one cares and is more worried about being on top than reality, where do we go from here? In my darkest time, someone said I am too real, and my response was, "It has been rough lately and all I have is reality." If there is no way to live, what is going on? Fifty to one hundred fifty million people need solutions. (These frustrations are mainly with the politicians in Washington and their budget gridlock from 2011-2013). I just wanted my country back on track so I could get my life back.

The saving grace is this is just a bad time in American history that we are all going through together. In that dark time, I needed some relief and the "50 Anti-Poverty States" were born. My mind came back to life and my heart felt warm. I felt like I could breathe again. My Great Recession songs "Shake Me Down" by Cage The Elephant and "Written In The Stars" by Tinie Tempah with Eric Turner, they meant so much more to me now.

I created this group of slogans to take the pressure off of myself. All that guilt, shame, and blame does nothing to solve this problem. In fact, it only keeps the problem going. I hope my "50 Anti-Poverty States of America" can bring some relief to you and your family as well.

The Great Recession wasn't my fault and it isn't your fault either. Sure I am responsible for my behavior and words but this is bigger than you or me! So I really have to lower my expectations for the future and on myself. We can relax with this new understanding and just breathe. Just breathe... Then take a minute to think about new jobs we can create. All jobs were created by someone's mind. What do you think your neighborhood or community needs?

This is a national disaster that historically happens to countries. The United States isn't immune from Recessions or Depressions. It has just been 70+ years since we had to go through something this bad again. Once we admit this, then we can do something about it. We are freed of its emotional grasp. Misery is not our natural state of being human.

If we need to point fingers we can easily look at predatory lenders in the housing crisis, Wall St. Executives, and the Banks from the Financial Collapse. We also need to hold our Government responsible for not putting white collar criminals in jail. We are all still feeling the sting of an Epic System Failure.

They say we need to aim for $18/hr. to start digging ourselves out of poverty. This equals a job paying 34 K. I have one suggestion in my book, "The Last Fill Up: Electric Bicycle Lifestyle Plans" that meets that goal, and it would be fun!

If I had had a job paying $34,000/yr. for the past 6 years none of this would have happened. **But it did**, and some very valuable "life lessons" have come out of it. I have found new ways to see our relationships with work, the city, and our nation. Napoleon Hill in the opening paragraph mentions "blessings" come along with economic depressions. Maybe this is what our country needed? Bad government policy and bad business practices can't go on unchecked forever.

I wanted to leave something for my fellow countrymen and women who are suffering right now with being broke, hungry, and living in insanity. I also don't want their children to go hungry either, that really bothers me. What's amazing is in the past we had the public, wealthy, spiritual groups, corporations, and politicians from the bottom to the top supporting programs to reverse this trend. This Great Recession has been different so far in its ignoring the people being impoverished. That is new. That is the difference between the last Gilded Age and this one, and why I am writing.

It is not an American value to exclude people or to prevent opportunities. **My frustrations are simply I do not understand why we are not helping each other MORE during the 2nd worst time in US history?** I am mad seeing that playing games is more important than starting solutions to curb poverty and the lack of employment. I think that is the real disaster of this Recession.

So now standing from the bottom of the rabbit hole, box, or well looking up, I'm an American who has fallen into poverty and The Great Recession. Now I can see both sides of the coin and what people have forgotten is, we are all equally human whether we have money or not. We all want the same things so let's help each other back up.

I am also a bicyclist and e-biker. What I love about bicycle culture is everybody is welcome and having fun while doing something good for the Earth, their health, and community. What has been nice to see is all economic classes have been getting into biking lately. I hope that same camaraderie can take part in new anti-poverty attitudes for the 21st Century.

After looking around at our US history, I really liked the Transcendental Movements attitude of the inherent goodness of both people and nature. Then we can add a 21st century spin on that. As long as you are learning, you can't fail, so overall you are going up! There is a good life we can all be part of with Interdependence. The USA has gone through this before and we can go through it again. Then I found current "real" answers.

There are 5 books that I would suggest to read. "The Rich and the Rest of US" by Tavis Smiley and Cornel West (Smiley & West, 2012). "The Great Divergence" by Timothy Noah (Noah, 2012). "How to Prosper In Hard Times" by the greatest motivational teachers of all times (Hill & Others, 2009). "Think and Grow Rich" by Napoleon Hill (Hill, 1937). "Three Feet From Gold" by Sharon Lechter and Greg Reid (Lechter & Reid, 2009). I feel those books will lay a good foundation for a strong attitude with our New American situation. Take a quick read through them and then re-read them again. There is hope here.

I found an interview on Youtube with the historian Niall Ferguson. He is a Professor of History at Harvard University and believes America will innovate. That is what we do and in ten years we'll be back. So we can get ready for better times in 2017. (Ferguson, 2009) We do have the resources, creativity, and manpower to do this. How are we really going to do that though?

I believe my "50 Anti-Poverty States of America" are a great place to begin. I have used it to focus on one or two slogans per day to snap out of it. No one needs to stay depressed over a lack of money. Depression can't hit a moving target so I focus on these while up and going about my day. I am also implementing the new wealth consciousness principles from the books listed. Can't wait to see what comes from it. My life lesson from all of this is, poverty is not a mental deficiency, lack of morality, or choice, it is simply a lack of money or work.

Oppression and the effects of oppression are a different story. I think this is what most people confuse with poverty. Since this Great Recession doesn't discriminate, oppression has hit everyone then. If you feel you are being discriminated against in the job hiring process, seek your local labor laws. The United States is a multi-cultural polytheistic society. Our culture and our laws can protect US from lack of work.

Now, we are at a turning point from this Great Recession. Everyone got thrown down except for the super-rich. I feel the general public is much stronger, more resilient, and more innovative than they know. I like the new 21st Century attitude of shifting from (why me?) to (what for?). So the last question becomes, will we continue the denial and silent suffering for broke Americans or will we work together and help each other out of hunger and poverty?

On this morning's radio show in April of 2013; 93.7 FM WCOL. A suburb of Columbus was asking for support of its food shelter. The Healthy Worthington Resource Center & Food Pantry said, "Childhood hunger rates are approaching 30%", in that idyllic town that US Presidents visit. I don't like knowing that possibly, 3 out of every 10 children I would see on the street there; aren't eating right because of the Recession and these new work trends. They called in to see if the listeners could help them?

Yes, I believe we can and that was another reason why I wrote this book. If this is going to be the new normal and we may not be able to get back to where we were. I wanted to be able to give back. I wanted to be able to help provide food for the charities or agencies that have helped me and the children sitting next to me at those church dinner tables as well. There are so many good hard working Americans that have gotten a raw deal lately and don't deserve to go hungry. Let's work together to better these new trends.

If you have liked the message of my book, "The 50 Anti-Poverty States of America", tell a friend, and then we can provide another $1 to a local or national food charity. Thank you for your time and thank you for helping to end hunger and poverty in America.

Conclusion

If we think about it, the ship already caught fire and sank in September of 2008, but is money the only thing that makes America great? No, I don't think so. So now we can all start working together to get out of these tough economic times. I hope I could show you that the Great Recession and new Gilded Age was not you're doing. This is a complex situation and because of that we can take the pressure off of ourselves, our co-workers, and community.

I believe, as long as we can produce jobs and re-train workers to fill those positions, we can get out of poverty. This is especially possible because the US has one of the top two highest worker productivity rates in the world. The "50 Anti-Poverty States of America" reminded me that I may be broke lately but I am not broken.

Hopefully, I could help dispel some of the myths about 21st Century poverty. I hope it could bring some emotional relief and "sugar" to you. The middle class and broke Americans are all going through this same experience now. Everyone can begin to help turn the Great Recession and these new work trends around, from bottom to top. It has been historically proven to be possible and true. Let's see where the "50 Anti-Poverty States of America" can take US.

- J.M. Seligman

Reference List and Suggested Readings

Websites
Teaching American History-National Politics In The Gilded Age 1873-1986. (2013), University of Nebraska
Retrieved March 23, 2013, from
http://www.tahg.org

I Hear America Singing: The American Renaissance & Transcendentalism (2013)
Hampson, T. Retrieved March 25, 2013, from
http://www.pbs.org

The Eleanor Roosevelt Papers Project:
The Progressive Era 1890-1920 (1904)
Roosevelt, E. Retrieved March 31, 2013, from
http://www.gwu.edu

Paiken, Steve (2009). Interview with Niall Ferguson On The Financial Crisis. Youtube, May 7, 2009.

Retrieved March 26, 2013 from
http://www.youtube.com/watch?v=By8nORkmzik

List of United States Cities By Population (2011).
July 1, 2011 by the United States Census Bureau.
Retrieved March 25, 2013
http://en.wikipedia.org/wiki/List_of_United_States_
cities_by_population

Books
Twain, M. & Warner, C.D. (1873). *The Gilded Age:
A Tale of Today*. New York: Penguin Books

Smiley, T. & West, C. (2012). *The Rich And The
Rest Of US*. New York: SmileyBooks
Noah, T. (2012). *The Great Divergence: America's
Growing Inequality Crisis And What We Can Do
About It*. New York: Bloomsbury Press

Hill, N. (1937). *Think And Grow Rich*. Chatsworth,
CA: Wilshire Book Company

Hill, N. & Allen, J. & Murphy, J. & Clason, G.S. &
Others (2009) *How To Prosper In Hard Times:
Blueprints For Abundance By The Greatest
Motivational Teachers Of All Time*.
New York: Tarcher/Penguin

Lechter, S. & Reid, G. (2009). *Three Feet From
Gold*
New York: Sterling Publishing Company

Newspaper or Online Articles

Berger, M. (2007, August 13). Brooke Astor, 105, First Lady of Philanthropy, Dies. *New York Times* [national ed.], Obituaries

Seman Jr., G. (2012, March 23). Artists Find Inspiration On COTA Bus Rides. *German Village Gazette* [national ed.],

Luhby, T. (2013, April 1). Wages Stink At Americas Most Common Jobs. *CNNMoney [online]*. Retrieved April 2, 2013, from http://money.cnn.com/2013/04/01/news/economy/jobs-wages/index.html?source=yahoo_hosted

About The Author

J.M. Seligman interests include bicycle and electric bike cultures, martial arts, holistic health and wellness, fitness, US and World Art and Culture. He has lived in Pittsburgh, Chicago, El Paso/Las Cruces, Philadelphia, Columbus, New York City, and Merida, Mexico to continue his education in the visual arts, writing, and the environment.

He was invited to perform at the New Mexico Taos Poetry Circus while participating in the El Paso Tumblewords Project. J.M. has performed at Chicago's Green Mill.

Currently he lives in Columbus and performs at local open mic nights including the Travonna Poetry Night and Kafe Kerouac Poetry Slam. He has joined the ranks of the American unemployed on and off again, since 2007, when The Great Recession began.

J.M. is a Volunteer with the Mid-Ohio Food Bank which is a branch of Feeding America. $1 of proceeds from every book goes to the Mid-Ohio Food Bank (local) and Feeding America (national) to fight hunger.

To Contact J.M. Seligman for readings or workshops:

Website: www.fiftyantipovertystates.org

Blog: joshuamseligman.blogspot.com

Twitter: @JM_Seligman

T-Shirts: www.skreened.com/bluedeer

It would be great to hear from you and how you are getting through this Great Recession and these new work trends. Go to my website or blog and leave a quote or paragraph from your "real life" experience. What personal triumphs have you had during these tough times? Join a community of individuals who are offering their hand up.

BONUS CHAPTER!
Go to www.fiftyantipovertystates.org and hit "Contact Me" to request the chapter excluded from "The 50 Anti-Poverty States of America". It is available as my gift to you.

Thank You!